enlist,
train,
support
church leaders

EVELYN M. HUBER

JUDSON PRESS, Valley Forge

ENLIST, TRAIN, SUPPORT CHURCH LEADERS

Copyright © 1975
Judson Press, Valley Forge, PA 19481

Unless otherwise indicated, Bible quotations in this volume are in accordance with the Revised Standard Version of the Bible, copyright © 1946 and 1952 by the Division of Christian Education of the National Council of the Churches of Christ in the United States of America, and are used by permission.

Library of Congress Cataloging in Publication Data

Huber, Evelyn.
  Enlist, train, support church leaders.

  Includes bibliographical references.
  1. Christian leadership. I. Title.
BV652.1.H8   254   74-22521
ISBN 0-8170-0667-2

Printed in the U.S.A. ⊕

contents

1
your
leadership
strategy

A letter writer by the name of Peter challenged an early Christian church with, "You are a chosen race, . . . God's own people, that you may declare the wonderful deeds of him who called you out of darkness into his marvelous light" (1 Peter 2:9)—a chosen people with a mission.

To the church at Ephesus, Paul wrote that God's gifts were ". . . that some should be apostles, some prophets, some evangelists, some pastors and teachers, for the equipment of the saints, for the work of ministry, for building up the body of Christ" (Ephesians 4:11-12).

These two New Testament pictures of the churches—the people of God with a mission and individual members with gifts for ministry—speak to the concern for leader development in the church today. They also suggest the goal for the training of leaders. The church is called to train the "people of God" for ministry.

All who respond to God's call to discipleship today, as of old, are charged with ministry. We are ordained to that ministry when we are baptized. The ministry of a church is only as effective as the members accepting the function of leadership make it.

How a church can go about helping persons respond to God's call to ministry and how it can help develop their leadership skills for a more effective ministry are what this book is all about. The book tries to share what some churches have learned through experience about selecting, recruiting, training, and supporting leaders. Its intent is to provide guidelines that may be helpful to your church.

The Starting Point

The leadership needs of a church grow out of its planning to fulfill its mission. Each program or ministry calls for leaders with particular qualifications or specialized skills. The specific kind of training needed will be determined by the program, the leaders selected, and their particular needs identified. A diagram of this progression is:

Mission→Leaders Selected → Leaders Enlisted→Leaders Trained and Supported

This book does not attempt to give guidelines to a church for defining its mission and program planning. It will deal with leadership for program.

Each church will develop its own processes for selecting, recruiting, training, and supporting its required leaders. If these tasks are to be done effectively, a church must develop an overall strategy to meet its leadership needs. Such an overall strategy will include:

- a definition of leadership and who a leader is
- a process for identifying the leadership needs as related to program
- a criteria for selecting leaders
- a plan for enlisting leaders
- a strategy for training and supporting leaders
- a program for the interpretation of the "leadership strategy" to the congregation and the selected leaders
- a process of assessment and evaluation.

What Is Leadership?

Leadership is a function. In the church, leadership is exercised by different people and in different ways. The leadership roles may be in planning, administration, teaching, guiding groups, or membership on a board, committee, or task force. These are all roles which enable others to be involved in growing in ministry or service.

Leadership is the responsibility an individual has for securing cooperation among members of a group or organization toward the achievement of a goal. It is concerned with the discovery and coordination of the members' resources. Persons usually take on a leadership role in a group because their concern and personal objectives coincide with the concerns and objectives of the group.

What a church believes about leadership is an important issue. It is important that each congregation clarify what it regards as important about leaders and leadership. This task of development can be entrusted to a small group and then shared with the congregation.

5

This small group may be the church council or advisory board, the nominating committee, the board of education, or a task force appointed by the pastor or one of the groups above.

Below are some statements about leadership. You probably will agree with some and disagree with others. Use these statements to help you clarify what you believe about leadership.

Leadership for the Christian is:

- responsible service as a response to the gospel.
- exercised in each situation as the individual sees the need. For the Christian, it is personal accountability to the total Christian community, the church.
- the exercise of power and influence in interaction with other persons.
- an expression of one's whole style of life. It may be aggressive, timid, democratic, autocratic, or laissez-faire.
- the exercise of personal aptitudes as well as skills that can be learned.
- the ability to express one's own convictions as well as to enable others to express theirs.

Who Is a Leader?

We often hold a narrow concept of who a leader is. Too often we think that only those assigned a designated leadership responsibility in some part of the church's program and ministry are leaders. These special leadership roles are important. But the concept of leadership is broader than this special function. A leader is a person who has influence over another person or group. While that person's influence is being felt, that person is leading. Individual church members often have not realized or accepted the concept that whenever they do anything or say anything which influences another person or a group, they are performing a leadership role. When a person affirms another's action, that person is acting as a leader. When a person encourages another person or a group to action or suggests a plan of action, he or she is a leader. When a person enables another to learn or teaches something to another, that person is a leader.

If they understand that much of what they already do is leadership, some persons may more easily accept designated leader roles. That all persons are potentially leaders is an important concept to be conveyed to the congregation.

For the welfare of the church, it is very important to consider the kinds of persons you are looking for. The persons or groups responsible for selecting designated leaders will wish to establish some guidelines. These criteria will reflect what the church values in persons who give leadership. These criteria should be shared with the congregation.

Once criteria have been established, they occasionally need to be evaluated and reaffirmed or changed to be in line with new understandings about the church, ministry, and human potential.

Each church will develop its own criteria. The following list of eighteen characteristics can stimulate a church's thinking. It was prepared by a group studying the question of the kind of leaders needed in the church's educational ministry. These characteristics are listed in two categories—general characteristics for all leaders and specific qualities for educational leaders. The order in which the characteristics are listed does not suggest an order of priorities.

General characteristics for church leaders

- is committed to Jesus Christ
- helps a group establish a climate of trust, openness, frankness
- gives time and energy to train for a leadership task
- helps a group set its own goals and organize to reach its goals
- sees the potential in others
- attends worship services and church activities
- is willing to accept and use other persons' points of view
- has high regard for oneself and is able to assess own strengths and limitations
- acts out of Christian commitment in all avenues of life.

Specific qualities for educational leaders

- gives information in an interesting way
- has a deep respect for the Bible
- involves the group in making decisions about its life and study
- plans sessions well ahead and has materials ready
- is able to express own beliefs
- understands how persons learn
- helps members of the group to learn from their own experiences
- is willing to use recommended materials
- knows how to listen to others.

The board, committee, council, or task force dealing with the concept of leadership will be able to build a list which reflects your church's views.

Why Be a Leader?

Motivation is the key to a person's accepting leadership. The desire

7

to serve in a leadership role comes from several sources. First, it may be affected by one's involvement in the church and the satisfaction with that involvement in the past. Persons may remember with some affection a church school teacher or youth group leader who had confidence in them and helped them to grow. This memory can motivate an individual to become involved with youth or children or parents now.

Second, one's present involvement in the church has some bearing on motivation for leadership. If persons like the kind of leadership role they have and feel their work is appreciated, their motivation for continued leadership is higher.

A third source of motivation for members of churches or other voluntary organizations is a sense of ownership of the goals of the group. Motivation is greater when there is opportunity to make decisions and solve problems. Persons who feel their voices have been heard in setting objectives and planning programs are more willing to serve on boards, committees, or task forces, or to teach. When members are heard to say "our program," "our mission," there is evidence that they really "own" the program and are willing to work. When the sense of ownership among members is lacking, participation usually falls off, financial support lags, and plans are not implemented. When there is not a sense of ownership, some people may even rebel or withdraw.

A fourth motivational factor for leadership is for persons to find that what they are asked to do meets their own personal needs and offers an opportunity to them for further personal growth and development.

What people believe or value affects their motivation. For example, if the Christian nurturing role is highly valued, accepting a leader role in the teaching ministry will be seen as important. For instance, parents who value a good Christian education for their children are more likely to give leadership.

And most important of all, motivation for leadership in the church depends on the person's own personal commitment to Jesus Christ and the belief that the church, as the Christian community, is called to communicate the healing gospel to a hurt world. If the leadership task seems relevant to that commitment and belief, acceptance of responsibility will be a challenge.

Another important factor in the motivation of leaders is the creation of a climate of excitement about leadership, whether it is in Christian education, in administration as a member of a board or committee, or in directing a neighborhood program.

How Does a Church Find Leaders?

The church is not just a leader and a group of followers. If a church is to meet its mission, all of the "gifts" of all the members are needed. These "gifts" are shared by individuals, both informally and through designated roles. An apt illustration here is a concept from Paul in his letter to the Corinthians:

> Now there are varieties of gifts, but the same Spirit; and there are varieties of service, but the same Lord.
> For just as the body is one and has many members, and all the members of the body, though many, are one body so it is with Christ.
> Now you are the body of Christ and individually members of it (1 Corinthians 12:4-5, 12, 27).

No church has all of the leaders it can use, but every church has leaders. There may be more leaders in your church than some people think. It is helpful to share with the congregation the characteristics of the kind of persons who are considered leader material.

Start the process of finding leaders before the deadline time arrives. Keep up-to-date records on all of the members of the church, and utilize the information about the skills and interests of the members as a source for potential leaders. This process will be discussed in Chapter 2.

Church Leaders as Volunteers

The concept of voluntarism and its relationship to lay persons' involvement in the church is often neglected. The gospel places the demand on lay persons to be "full-time" Christians. It calls them to active ministry as they live out their commitment to Jesus Christ in the family, at work, and in the community, as well as in the church. Their use of energy, abilities, and time will be determined by what they consider to be important. In the sense that lay persons determine how much time they will give in the maintenance of church boards and committees or in Christian education roles, they are volunteers. The fact that they are volunteers affects how much time they will give in the performance of their roles. It will determine how much support they need as they carry out their leader roles. It often affects how they view the task of the church's professional leadership.

Much is currently being written regarding the role of voluntarism in today's society. It would be well for the professional leadership of a church and perhaps those lay leaders who are concerned with the selection, recruitment, development, and support of volunteers to read some of the substantive pieces in the field. The issues raised may be studied and discussed while developing a plan for selecting, training, and supporting leaders.

Your Church's Leadership Strategy

The format suggested here is one way to plan a church's leadership strategy.

The various groups and persons who are involved in program planning will need to help in the response to question 5 as suggested here.

Questions	Our Church's Response	
1. What is the purpose or mission goal of our church?		
2. What are some important beliefs our church has about who a leader is and what leadership is?	1. 2. 3. 4.	
3. What is being done, or will be done, to highlight your leadership needs and motivate persons to accept leadership roles?	1. 2. 3. 4.	
4. List the leadership qualities selected for leaders. How will these be shared with prospective leaders and the entire congregation?		
5. Based on your mission goal, what programs for which leaders are needed have been planned for the year?	**Program** 1. 2. 3. 4.	**Number and kinds of leaders needed**

2
enlist
leaders

There comes that time each year in every congregation when the question, "Who will take each leadership responsibility this year?" has to be answered.

The first step in enlisting leaders is the selection of those who are best qualified to fill each specific leadership task. The selection process starts when each program is determined and the leaders needed are identified. It is helpful if a very brief description of the task is written out. Also it should be stated how long the person will be asked to serve—three years, one year, six months.

The second step is filling each leadership need with the best qualified person available. The progression is illustrated in the diagram below:

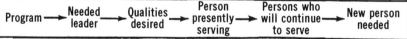

There is added value in looking at the strengths of the persons already on a board, committee, or teaching team. New personnel can be selected to balance and strengthen the groups. It is wise, if possible, to keep a balance between persons with experience and those who are inexperienced.

Who Makes the Selection?

One group representing all of the ministries and programs of the church should coordinate the selection of leaders. This group will constantly ask what leadership qualities and potential each prospective leader has. Such a group can avoid the mad scramble to find leaders two months before the annual meeting or the beginning of the fall teaching-learning session.

Early selection avoids overlooking some potential leaders or the possibility that some dynamic persons may be pressured by too many requests. It also avoids a sense of competition for leadership by the various groups, boards, and committees. Another plus to having all leaders selected by one group is that prospective leaders have more freedom to look at options. This selection group will work closely with each board or committee or supervisory personnel so that a brief description of each job may be written before the recruiting process is started. This same group will initiate and supervise the maintenance of a personnel file.

This selection task may suggest a different job description for the nominating committee than has usually been the case. Or it may call for the appointment of a new group which would work in cooperation with the nominating committee and church boards and groups.

An *information file* preserves a reservoir of information about potential leaders as well as present leaders. When a record system is set up, it needs to be very simple and easily updated. Record only the most important essentials, such as name, address, telephone number, occupation, past experience, present leadership roles in church and community, special interests, gifts, skills, and training.

Some churches keep their listing by program categories. Others record the skills, understandings, and information needed in the various roles and catalog the prospective leaders' names in the categories they are able to fill. A variety of already prepared forms are available from denominational bookstores. Keep the file accessible and in a form easily used.

Enlisting Leaders

After the selection of leaders is made, the invitation to serve is personally extended. The most appropriate means for enlisting each person needs to be chosen. Lay persons need to be involved in enlisting other lay persons in order to dramatize the importance of lay involvement in the congregation.

Who does the enlisting?

Planning for the enlistment of leaders is done by the same coordinating group which made the selection. However, the actual invitation is extended by persons who are knowledgeable about the task and who can best present the opportunity in a positive manner. Let us use the educational leaders as an illustration. The board of Christian education has been represented on the coordinating group which makes the leadership selection. The leaders needed for the educational programs have been presented along with the qualities they need. The board will work with this group in planning the enlistment. The enlistment may be done by another member of the teaching team, one or more board members, the church school superintendent, or the pastor. Members of the group or class (especially in youth and adult groups) may be the best qualified to do the enlisting.

How are leaders enlisted?

There are a variety of ways to interpret leadership needs and offer the invitation to leadership. Some methods will be more appropriate at one time than another. Some will be more appropriate to one church than another. Remember that a carefully planned contact will lend importance and significance to the enlistment effort. Experience shows that such an approach produces a high proportion of positive results.

The most effective method is to recruit on a one-to-one basis or by a team of two persons contacting the prospective leader. The prospect's home is often an ideal setting. A telephone call or a quick conference on the way to a worship service is the least effective approach. The effective contact takes time.

Another method for recruitment is to bring the prospective leaders together in an informal setting for a meeting. When invited to attend, prospects can be told what position it is hoped they will accept or whether there is a choice between·two tasks. The church's leadership needs are presented to the total group. The criteria used for selecting leaders are shared. Present leaders share their hopes and dreams for the church. The prospective leaders have an opportunity to ask questions. Those being recruited are given the opportunity to indicate a willingness to serve.

In recruiting educational leaders it is helpful for the prospective leader to meet the group or observe in the group he or she may be working with.

Regardless of the method used, some important guidelines need to be followed:
- Be warm and open.
- Share the church's criteria for the selection of leaders so that the prospect will know why he or she was selected and what the church expects of leaders.

- Indicate how long the person is expected to serve.
- Inform the prospects whom they will be working with and explain the relationship.
- Explain the process for evaluation of the leader's work.
- Provide an opportunity for the prospect to express his or her feelings, hopes, concerns, and personal needs and to ask questions.
- Explore how already developed skills can be used, and assure the prospect that special training is available if needed.
- Give the person all materials which would be helpful, such as curriculum resources, or indicate that this will be provided.
- Let the individual be free to say "no." Persevere but do not pressure.

It is important that the person being recruited perceives the service as:
- needed
- interesting
- worthwhile
- an opportunity to keep growing personally.

If the prospect wishes time to think about the invitation, set a date when a response will be expected.

There may be some persons who have all the qualities your church is looking for in a leader but lack some of the leadership skills. Or there are some persons who are perceived as having the skills and qualities, but they are not sufficiently sure of themselves to take on a task. Plan for a program of personal counseling, encouragement, and evaluation to give these persons confidence and the skill training that they feel they need.

Once the leadership roles are filled for one year, start preparing for the next. Keep the leadership needs of the church constantly before the congregation. When the immediate pressure is off, there is opportunity for more relaxed cultivation and development of leadership potential.

Your Church's Plan for Selecting and Enlisting Leaders

Below is a suggested plan for use in planning for this year.

Questions	Our Church's Response
1. Has a job description been developed for each job, outlining what the task is and what is expected of the leaders?	
2. If job descriptions have not been prepared, who will do each one and by what date?	
3. What method will be used for recruitment of leaders?	(Describe)

4. Who will contact each person and when?	Leader's Name	Contact Person	Date Decision Needed

3
train
leaders

Leader development in the church is educating the laity in the theological concept that they are "God's people" and they have a ministry to fulfill. Leader training educates so that persons can use their influence wisely and usefully. Developing and training leaders is meeting persons where they are and enabling them to use their gifts more effectively in order to move the church to new positions of strength and influence.

If it is true that leaders are not born but are developed, then developing and training the laity for leadership will be a high priority for a church. It will be planned as an integral part of the total Christian education program of the church. Each youth and adult class or group should have training for leadership functions as one objective. Leader development integrated into the Christian education of the church means that children, youth, and adults are encouraged to see leadership in the church as a positive, satisfying experience. They will be helped to see that leaders serve on behalf of the congregation and to appreciate such service.

A Plan for Leader Training

Providing your leaders with opportunities for personal growth and skill training is the best support your church can give them. Knowing how to do the task and having a personal sense of growing helps to keep leaders from becoming discouraged and giving up.

The leader training program should also include training for potential leaders. As the committee or group responsible for recruitment continually seeks possible new leaders, the training committee will provide enrichment and study opportunities for these potential leaders, including training in any needed special skills.

A church will have some long-range development and training goals which will lead the church toward the ideal. These long-range goals will be developed on the basis of what the church believes about leaders and their leadership needs. One church set as its long-range goal the objective that every person taking a leadership role would receive the necessary skill training to perform satisfying service and the learning opportunities for personal development. The first short-range goal in relation to the long-range goal was to conduct a retreat which centered on individual growth. The next year an objective was added related to skill training. Another church set as its long-range goal the objective of developing a corps of persons who would be able and willing to train others in the skills of teaching, planning, or chairing boards and committees. Their first short-term objective led them to have one teacher in each age group department trained as a "master" teacher who would train other teachers in that department.

Out of your goals will come your strategy or plan for training and development. The basics to be included in the plan are:

- the identification of a group to be responsible for the training program
- opportunity for leaders to identify leadership training needs
- progression and growth in the training opportunities provided
- inclusion of potential leaders as well as present leaders in training plans.

Your plan will respond to these questions.

- Is it necessary? Have the leaders received this kind of training elsewhere? For instance, has the person received training in his/her employment that can be used?
- Does it take into account existing leadership? Can leaders already involved train new leaders in the process of serving together? Does the existing leadership need to be retrained?
- Is it the kind of training where the participant learns from experience? Perhaps a warning is in order: do not try to do the whole task at once. A well planned course of training, part of which is achieved each year, may be a more feasible plan.

Who Is Responsible?

One group needs to have responsibility for developing and

implementing the leader training program. While it may not be traditional, more and more churches are seeing that the board or committee of Christian education has responsibility for the training of all church leaders, not just the educational leaders. This group has experience in leader training. It usually has in its membership persons who understand education. Therefore, it may be time for your board or committee of Christian education to broaden its base of responsibility.

If a church has several people who have expertise in education and skill training, it might want a separate task force on training. Such a task force would work cooperatively with all boards and be accountable to all boards and committees through the church council or advisory board.

Leaders Identify Needs

Plan the training from the perspective of the ones being trained. They should be involved in the early stages of developing the training program by identifying their training needs. They understand their own needs best. They will have a keener interest in the training if they are consulted and see it meeting their needs.

There are a variety of ways in which training needs can be assessed.

Checklists may be useful. A sample of two is given here. Checklist A is specifically slanted toward educational leaders. It can be adapted for use by other boards and committees. Checklist B is specifically aimed at board and committee chairpersons but can be adapted to teachers and group leaders.

In a small church, each new leader may be interviewed regarding training needs and interest. This process is very helpful when it is feasible. The checklists suggest some of the kinds of questions which can be used in the interviews.

CHECKLIST A: SKILL RATING FOR EDUCATIONAL LEADERS

For each teacher or leader to complete:

1. **Rank the following skills in the order of their importance to you as a teacher/leader.** (1 is the most important—13 is the least important.)

_____Being able to ask questions clearly and specifically.

_____Planning a teaching-learning session or group meeting.

_____Using a variety of methods or learning activities.

_____Providing the opportunity for class action and involvement in mission.

_____Being able to understand what another person is saying.

_____Discovering the interests and needs of group members.

_____Responding to persons with positive reinforcement (praise, affirmation, acceptance of feelings, etc.)

_____Leading Bible study.

_____Conducting evaluation.

_____Using the teaching-learning resources in the class/group.

_____Using students' opinions and suggestions.

_____Involving the members of the group with self in planning, experiencing, and evaluating a session together.

_____Others_____

_____

2. **Mark "X" to indicate three or four of these skills that you would like to work on during the coming year.**

3. **Check the following areas of information in which you would like help.**

   a. ( ) Understanding what the Bible is and how it came to be.
   b. ( ) Understanding the characteristics of:
               ( ) children   ( ) youth   ( ) adults.
   c. ( ) Understanding the religious readiness of children.
   d. ( ) Understanding the role of the teacher.

CHECKLIST B: DEFINE YOUR TRAINING NEEDS AS A LEADER

1. Think about your group/committee or board and the meetings you conduct with them. What do you most want to happen? Write your wish here.

2. List the skills and information you think you need in order to work more effectively to make your wish come true.

3. Rank the above skills and information in order of importance to you. Number 1 will be of most importance. Put an "X" in front of the ones that you feel you need to develop. If there are more than three, circle the three you wish to work on this year.

Another suggestion for a plan to help leaders define their training needs is one a church used when the leaders came to an orientation meeting. All leaders were asked to respond to the three questions below:

- List problems you face in the leadership responsibility.
- Write expectations or personal goals you have for your task.
- List the resources you bring. From your background and

training, identifv knowledge, skills, and talents which will help you reach these goals and solve your problems.

A group list was compiled for each question. Where there was need and few or no resources to meet that need, it was decided training would be given.

A church's strategy for leader development will allow for opportunity to move from one level of learning to the next. Start with the basics. Provide what the leader needs to know to get started. These needs usually are at the skill level. Your plan for educating leaders will not stop there. There is content to be mastered. There are human relations skills to be learned which help in relating and interacting with others. There is the need for all leaders to understand themselves better.

Models for Training

A variety of training models is possible. The one used will depend on the type of leadership roles and the training needs of the leaders. One model may not meet all the needs and the various degrees of experience. Described here are a few experience-centered models.

Workshops

In workshops there are general sessions and face-to-face groups. In the general sessions the workshop leader usually gives information and guides the learning. In the face-to-face groups the participants become resources to each other and work together on what is to be learned. The choice of the word "workshop" is not accidental. It implies that persons work at their own learning. They are involved in the process. Workshops are usually one day or longer or a series of shorter sessions tied together with a common objective.

A workshop is a good model for:

- learning skills
- learning group functions
- learning to use creative activities.

Laboratory training

In laboratory training, persons can try out teaching or leading a group. Skilled leader(s) is (are) present who can give guidance. The learners also receive valuable help developing their skills in teaching or leading from the other participants. In a laboratory, persons can test new skills and improve their use of new methods in leading before trying them in their own churches.

Laboratories are usually five to ten days in length. They are best conducted away from home so that participants are not distracted by personal or business responsibilities. Laboratory training is very helpful in learning to work with a specific age group or in learning and practicing leadership skills.

Seminars

A seminar is made up of persons who have studied an issue and prepared and shared papers on it. Others not involved in preparing the papers can be present and learn from the reading and discussion of the material. Persons learn from each other.

A seminar is best used when a small group of people wish to study an issue and clarify their thinking by sharing. A seminar can be conducted on issues like theology, ecology, social justice, community and world missions, or age group characteristics.

Observation

This is an especially good model for educational leaders. A teacher or group leader can learn by observing another leader at work in a group or class. Observation can be done in a public school, in another church, or in one's own church. Two teachers can team up for this kind of training by taking turns learning from each other.

Observing another class can help one to:

- discover new ways of teaching
- improve teaching skills, such as question asking, student-teacher and student-student relationships, etc.
- gain self-confidence in own ability
- enlarge one's concept of teaching and the skills needed.

If a church has video tape equipment or a cassette tape recorder, or can borrow one, these may be used to improve leadership abilities. A session is taped and then played back. By observing oneself, a leader can identify what was done well and what skills need to be improved. The teacher or leader can invite another teacher to view the video tape or listen to the cassette and make suggestions. Video taping or tape recording a committee meeting and reviewing the recording is a good way for that group to learn better ways of working together. Guidelines such as what helped and what hindered the group work should be used in reviewing the tapes.

Teams of teachers

An experienced leader can work with an inexperienced leader in a team relationship. The inexperienced leader asks and receives feedback on his/her performance of the task. The experienced leader teaches needed skills to the inexperienced leader. This method is especially useful in training educational leaders.

Tutors

A trained teacher or leader can tutor another person. Skills especially can be taught this way. Some of these skills are session planning, use of creative learning activities, evaluation, how to ask questions, storytelling, and discussion leading.

If a teacher has many teaching skills but feels a lack of biblical background, the pastor has an excellent opportunity to become tutor in this area.

The pastor often takes on the tutor role with new board chairpersons helping them learn good group and administrative skills.

Consultant

Consultation is not giving advice or supplying answers. The consultant asks questions rather than gives information. Consultation is a process of diagnosis and problem solving. The consultant leaves the individual with a process which can be used to solve other problems. A teacher experiencing a problem with a particular child in the class can be helped to find a better approach. Or a teacher might have problems with the use of curriculum resources. A consultant, listening and asking questions, can help the teacher to understand better the resources and their potential use. The pastor often is called upon to do this. The pastor is also a good consultant for a board or committee on how to plan and work.

Resources for Training

There are many resources, both printed and audiovisual, available to local congregations. There is sufficient variety that a local church can tailor-make training offers to meet the specific needs of its particular leaders each year. A listing of many of these is given in the appendix of this book.

Persons as resources

A congregation often has one or more persons who, because of special training in their businesses or professions, are capable of training others. Such persons include public school teachers, supervisors, managers, business executives, personnel directors, or persons in organizational development programs in mental health agencies or community organizations.

The pastor is a valuable resource in training. The pastor may be able to train board and committee personnel in better ways of conducting meetings, agenda setting, group process, use of the Bible in teaching, etc.

Don't overlook persons in the community who have training skills or who are members of other churches. Often they can be enlisted for short-term training programs. It is usually better for several small churches to plan for leader training together so that the especially gifted leaders in a community or church are not asked for more time than they have to give.

National denominational offices can consult by mail; and regional, state, or city denominational staff are willing to provide leader training as time permits.

If persons who are not members of the congregation are asked to give training, it may be necessary to offer an honorarium or pay travel, room, and meal costs.

Junior colleges and state universities are often willing to provide training opportunities for church leaders. Sometimes courses in the regular academic program are open to the public.

Budget

One of the most essential items in the church budget is that which covers the cost of training leaders. Since the budget represents money allocated for those things which are considered important, the amount designated for leader development and training indicates its priority. In the matter of developing a budget, long-range and short-term goals will play an important part.

* * *

On the following page you will find guidance for developing your church's plan for leader development and training.

Your Church's Plan for Leader Development and Training

Questions	Our Church's Response

1. Who are the persons or group of persons responsible for training leaders?

(Names)

2. What plan will we use in order that leaders can identify their training needs?

3. What is the budget for leader training?

4. What kind of training needs were identified and how will these be met?

Name of leader	Identified needs	Kind of training to be offered	When	Where

4
support
leaders

To accept a leadership task with high hopes and expectations and then to discover that nobody cares, not even the person who did the recruiting, is a disillusioning experience. A church in its master plan for selecting, recruiting, and developing leaders can avoid disillusionment by planning for support of these leaders. Such support says to the leaders, "We really care about you and what you do." Some support is informally given, such as a word of appreciation in passing on Sunday morning. However, a program of support needs to be planned in order to demonstrate that ministry belongs to the whole church. When leaders are seen as working on behalf of the church, a sense of loyalty to the leaders develops. A plan of support includes expressing appreciation for the persons giving leadership. Support by the total congregation indicates a mutual trust between the membership and the leaders. A supportive climate helps to release power and energy for work.

The plan of support will vary from church to church and sometimes will vary within a church from year to year. Use a variety of ways to offer support. Variety helps to keep the concept of support alive and fresh and therefore real.

Guidelines for Developing a Support Program

Orient leaders

Getting off to a good start is very important. An orientation session for leaders can prevent many frustrations. It is very evident that for maximum satisfaction all who are ministering in a leadership role must be committed to the same general mission goal. Remind the leaders of this goal. Leaders need to see where their particular task and its objectives fit into the overall goal of the church.

An orientation session for all leaders, including new leaders as well as those already serving, serves a variety of useful functions. Leaders need to know the avenues available for carrying out their responsibilities. Another value is the opportunity for leaders to know each other better. New leaders can hear about the satisfaction and the frustration of the others with whom they will be involved. This gives a realistic picture of the task. The new leaders have opportunity to understand more fully what is expected of them as the task is delineated. An orientation session also provides opportunity to instruct leaders in what are sometimes called the "housekeeping matters," such as procedures for securing supplies and resources, bill payments, and the meeting times of boards and committees. Orientation provides an opportunity to know where work is reported and how coordination takes place. Special regulations of the church should be explicitly described.

How the orientation session is conducted is important. A discussion or panel presentation by persons already involved in leadership will be more interesting than a presentation by one person. Keep details to a minimum. These can be put into writing and kept for future reference. The orientation session will include sharing, fellowship, and time for the individual boards, committees, and educational leaders to become acquainted. The professional leadership of the church, the pastor and other staff members, will be present to share in the orientation. Their presence gives opportunity to build a collaborative relationship between lay and professional leaders.

Recognize lay leaders publicly

One way of indicating support by the congregation and the professional leadership is provision for the whole church to say, "We stand along with you. We trust you. Thank you for what you do on our behalf." It is very encouraging to have good work appreciated. This recognition can be given within the context of the congregation at worship. Often it is given at the same time a service of dedication for leaders is conducted. In this context, the leaders dedicate their service and the congregation pledges its support.

In conjunction with the dedication and recognition service, a reception or coffee hour can be conducted. In this informal setting, individual members can get to know the leaders and express appreciation to them.

Provide resources

To plan a program and staff it with leaders but not provide budget, printed resources, films, pictures, facilities and equipment, etc., when needed is unwise. Educational leaders especially need many resources. Leaders should not be expected to pay for these resources. Leaders may be given a printed sheet providing information about who can operate the audiovisual equipment, what books are available, and where supplies are kept.

Offer learning opportunities and skill training

The possibility for learning never ends. One of the best means of support to leaders is training for the leadership task. If the lay leaders are developing their leadership potential, the whole church will be strengthened. Suggestions about training were given in Chapter 3. Resources for training are listed in the appendix.

Help leaders develop their own criteria for performance and check out their own achievement

Don't impose artificial standards. Help the leader to look at what really matters in the leadership role which has been accepted. Encourage the leader to set an individual goal for functioning in the role. This goal will be based on what the leader values in the task. It is helpful if the goal is shared with at least one person and the achievement of the goal is checked out occasionally with this person. If the goal or criteria for performance is shared, the leader not only makes a personal evaluation of performance but also has the opportunity for feedback from another person. This may be done with another member of the same board, committee, or teaching group. Encourage leaders to judge their work on the basis of what they value.

Provide an atmosphere of freedom to function

This atmosphere says that the congregation trusts the leader. Persons give of themselves best when they feel that they are helping make decisions which affect them. Being involved in decision making related to one's function as a leader is freeing.

Offer feedback on work rather than criticism

Criticism is often one person's opinion of how something should be

27

done. Feedback is given by persons closely related to the task. Feedback describes what was seen and heard and what the effect was. Feedback is given on what is observable, not on hearsay. It is best given when requested or when the person giving it has asked permission to give it.

To know that perfection is not a criterion for leadership frees persons to be more creative and to try new methods. A responsible leader will not take advantage of this freedom, but use it wisely for the benefit of the task and others.

Who Plans the Program of Support?

Planning for support of leaders is of concern to those who selected and enlisted them. The coordinating group will make these plans or assign the task to someone. The church council or advisory board might see this as an important responsibility. Leader support won't happen, though, unless it is lodged as the responsibility of some group.

Your Church's Plan for Supporting Your Leaders

Here is a suggested form for your use as you plan.

Questions	Our Church's Response
1. When and where will your orientation session for leaders be conducted? Who will be in charge? Describe the plan.	Date _____ Place _____ Names _____
2. What will be done to recognize publicly this year's leaders? When will recognition take place? Who will be in charge?	_____
3. Has each board and committee arranged for needed resources and supplies?	
4. What help will be given for developing individual performance standards? For letting leaders know how they are doing?	

28

5
and
finally . . .

Leader development is a long process—sometimes very long. But in order for a church to have all the leaders it needs, it must begin with a step-by-step plan. Now may be the time for your church to take a new look at who leaders are and how they are selected, enlisted, trained, and supported. Decide where you need to begin; then start.

A Warning and a Suggestion. Don't be too ambitious if you are just starting out. Select for each year that which can be achieved. Nonachievable plans are self-defeating. However, keep the long-range goal before the group responsible for planning and think big.

Evaluate periodically and build in new plans each year. When the present leaders see a developing plan which takes them seriously, they take new hope and they have stronger motivation for their task.

appendix
of
resources

Workshop Guides

The Teacher as Planner, Literature Service, Judson Book Stores, LS 15-618, price $5.00. The five guides in this packet are for use by persons planning local church training workshops for teachers and other educational leaders. Each guide has step-by-step guidance for the workshop leader. The focus of all workshops is on helping the teacher plan better.

The Teacher and the Bible, Literature Service, Judson Book Stores, LS 15-617, price $4.00. In this packet there are guides for three different workshops. One is for one session workshop and the other two are four sessions each.

Teaching Yourself to Teach, a Multimedia Self-Instruction Kit. Price $7.95. Developed through cooperation of Cooperative Publication Association and Project Committee on Vacation-Leisure Settings, of National Council of Churches.

Person to Person. Price $24.95. A kit of cassette tapes and workbooks for eight sessions. The workshops are for teachers on communicating, teaching, and learning through sight, sound, taste, and touch.

Developing Your Leadership Potential. Price $24.95. A kit of cassette tapes and work sheets for ten workshop sessions. Deals with basic leadership skills, motivation, creative teaching, and relating learning to life. Some sessions helpful to boards and committee.

Don't Be Afraid, 16 mm. color film. Rental $15.00 from American Baptist Films.* Shows several models for youth ministry. Excellent for motivating leadership.

Biblical Studies for Teachers. For suggestions of books and study guides write to: Department of Educational Planning Services, Board of Educational Ministries, American Baptist Churches, Valley Forge, PA 19481.

For Individual Study

Leader's Notebook. LS 12-122, price $1.75. Included is some of the guidance that teachers need to communicate effectively the Christian faith to children. There is also a selection for administrators with responsibilities in children's ministry.

Learning Is Change, Martha M. Leypoldt. Price $2.95. A book which outlines a process for adults to become involved in the learning process through exercises and reflection.

Youth Ministry: Sunday, Monday, and Every Day, John Carroll and Keith Ignatius. Price $1.65. Tells how to organize for youth ministry by first finding the needs of youth in the church.

Communicating with Junior Highs, Robert Browning. Price $1.95. How to listen to, learn from, and engage in dialogue with younger teens.
Partners in Teaching Young Children, Martha Locke Hemphill. Price $2.50.
Partners in Teaching Older Children, Lulu Hathaway. Price $2.50.

Priest to Each Other. Carlyle Marney. Price $2.95. Highlights that the right of priesthood remains with the people. Lay people are seen as those who will spread the gospel in the world.

Resources for Training Board and Committee Members

Planning Christian Education in Your Church. Kenneth D. Blazier and Evelyn M. Huber. Price $1.00. A step-by-step guide for those planning for education. Teaches the planning process while one is "doing it." Useful to other boards in planning.

The Person Who Chairs the Meeting. Paul O. Madsen. Price $1.95. A practical book for planning board meetings and conducting them.

Team Building in Church Groups. Nancy Geyer and Shirley Noll. Price $1.00. A guide on how individuals can work together to

*Valley Forge, PA 19481 or Box 23204, Oakland, CA 94623.

accomplish a common task and experience what it means to be "one body in Christ."

Church Meetings That Matter. Philip A. Anderson. Price $1.60. The book shows lay persons how they can put more into and get more out of the meetings they attend.

The Center Letter from the Center for Parish Development, 320 East School Avenue, Naperville, IL 60540. Published once each month. Each issue deals with some important phase of administrative and leadership role in the church. Subscription to *Center Letter* $3.00 per year.

Creative Problem Solving. First of the Leader-in-the-Box series. Price $19.95. Cassette tapes and workbooks for use by boards in planning their year's work.

Planning for Education in the Congregation, a multimedia kit. Price $20.00. Provides a planning process and tools for getting the needed information to tailor-make a church's program.

Further readings can be obtained through:

Leader Development Resource System, Board of Education, United Methodist Church, $4.95.

On Voluntarism

The Volunteer Community: Creative Use of Human Resources. Schindler-Rainman, Eva and Lippitt, Ronald. Price $5.00 Center for a Voluntary Society, National Training Laboratories, Institute for Applied Behavioral Science, 1507 M. Street Northwest, Washington, DC 20005.

Volunteers Today. Harriet H. Naylor. Price $5.50. Dryden Associates.

Volunteer Training and Development. A. K. Stenzel and H. M. Feeney. Price $5.95.